Short Moments
of Open Intelligence

Repeated Many Times, Become Continuous

The Most Powerful and Easy
Way to Live

Balanced View Team

Library of Wisdom Classics

Third Edition 2012
Balanced View Media: Mill Valley, California USA 2012

ISBN 978-0-9886659-2-7

Short Moments of Open Intelligence
Repeated Many Times, Become Continuous

Table of Contents

INTRODUCTION

Welcome to the Library of Wisdom Classics! We invite you to discover the incredible resource of your own innate open intelligence.

Open intelligence illuminates a vast treasure of power and benefit within humankind. It provides the greatest of riches. The treasure is contained in the phrase "short moments of open intelligence, repeated many times, become obvious and continuous."

Such a simple action actually has the great power to bring about complete mental and emotional stability, cooperation and peace within global human culture. This book contains vital knowledge that is essential to open intelligence, cooperation and peace.

The Library of Wisdom Classics series began with *One Simple Change Makes Life Easy* and continues with its companion book, *Short Moments of Open intelligence, Repeated Many Times, Become Obvious and Continuous.*

The talks that make up the fifteen chapters of this book were given by the founder of the Balanced View Training, Candice O'Denver, in 2008 in Sweden and the United States. All the talks were transcribed, edited and reviewed, and the resulting material became the basis for this book.

Heartfelt and gracious gratitude to Candice for this life-changing and inspiring training that ensures complete well-being for everyone and the power to be of benefit to all, and much thanks and acknowledgement for the outstanding assistance from so many volunteers who have made this wonderful book possible.

Enjoy this marvelous journey!

OPEN INTELLIGENCE IN DAILY LIFE

CHAPTER ONE

"The very first moment of open intelligence already has within it the result of complete relief, mental and emotional stability, power, deep caring, self-benefit and the benefit of all."

What is a short moment of open intelligence? To know the answer to that question, *stop thinking* just for a moment. What remains? A sense of alertness and clarity remains. This is the clarity of open intelligence. Clarity, open intelligence and awareness are synonymous.

Just as a rainbow appears within space, thoughts, emotions, sensations and other experiences appear within the clarity and alertness of open intelligence. Just as space and a rainbow are inseparable, thoughts, emotions, sensations and other experiences are inseparable from open intelligence.

When we stop thinking for a moment, we introduce ourselves to open intelligence, and before long we begin to notice that the open intelligence that is present when we are *not* thinking is also present when we *are* thinking. All thoughts appear and vanish naturally like the flight path of a bird in the sky.

The open intelligence and alertness that is identified when we stop thinking is the basis of all thoughts. It saturates all thoughts without exception. This is similar to the vastness of space being present regardless of what appears within it.

At the very moment data form, recognize always present open intelligence. A datum is anything that occurs within the all-encompassing view of open intelligence. It can be a thought, emotion, sensation or other experience, and it can relate to inner or outer events. Data within open intelligence can be likened to a breeze blowing through the air. The breeze and the air are inseparable. Both are air.

Like the color blue is inseparable from the sky, data are inseparable from open intelligence. We come to realize that no datum has an origin independent of open intelligence. Right now, look at your own experience to see if it is like that or not.

It makes no difference what data arise. In open intelligence, they vanish naturally, leaving no trace, like a line drawn in the sky. Open intelligence, relaxed and enormously potent, is the source of mental and emotional stability, insight and skillful qualities and activities. By the power of instinctive open intelligence these become increasingly evident.

Just rest the mind and body naturally, without seeking anything or pushing anything away. This is all that is required, whether activity is strenuous, relaxed or in-between. What remains is open intelligence that is open like a clear sky. This is what open intelligence is! When the next thought comes, it appears due to open intelligence. This is similar to the vast sky being present regardless of the presence of what appears within it.

OPEN INTELLIGENCE AND COMPLETE MENTAL AND EMOTIONAL STABILITY

Open intelligence, in the immediacy of the flow of thoughts, emotions and sensations, is the source of profound insight, a balanced view, complete mental and emotional stability, compassion and skillfulness in all situations. The innate ability to be at ease, wise, balanced and compassionate is discovered in open intelligence.

Because of the habit of emphasizing data, the initial brief moments of open intelligence may not last long at first. In other words, there may be no real stability. It may almost immediately slip away. This is perfectly fine. That is why short moments are repeated many times until open intelligence becomes obvious and continuous. This is the key point in gaining confidence in open intelligence.

At first we may remember to rely on open intelligence only once in a while. This is perfectly okay and is the way it is for most everyone. Initially we remember a short moment of open intelligence and then we forget. This is normal. However, we must not give up—ever!

We must not give up; these brief moments of open intelligence, as momentary as they are in the beginning, are having a tremendous impact. The benefits may not be so obvious initially. The key point is to stay interested in open intelligence. We must have this kind of resolve: "I will never give up on short moments of open intelligence, repeated many times, until it is obvious and continuous!"

The first time the choice is made to rely on open intelligence rather than emphasizing data, there is a sense of the great power of complete relief to be found in open intelligence. By persisting in this one simple choice, benefits are seen from the outset. The flow of data is not altered. Everything is left simply *as it is*. By the power of short moments of open intelligence, open intelligence becomes increasingly obvious.

The very first moment of open intelligence already has within it the result of complete relief, mental and emotional stability, power, deep caring, self-benefit and the benefit of all. By repeatedly relying on open intelligence, it becomes obvious. Short moments, many times, become obvious and continuous. This exceptionally potent method grants access to a powerful intelligence that is not noticed when there is emphasis on descriptions or data streams. So continue to take short moments of open intelligence, leaving everything *as it is*, whenever you remember to do so, until open intelligence is continuous at all times.

There is no reason to complicate open intelligence. As open intelligence is the basis of every perception, it is already naturally present. It isn't something that needs to be obtained sometime in the future. That's why the single instruction that is needed is "short moments, repeated many times." By taking a short moment of open intelligence, we ensure that it is uncontrived and natural.

FREEDOM IN IMMEDIATE PERCEPTION

Rather than trying to get into a state of not thinking and calling it "open intelligence," see that open intelligence is present in every perception, whether there is thinking or no thinking. This keeps it very simple. There is freedom in the immediate perception of "not thinking" as equally as there is freedom in the immediate perception of "thinking."

Another crucial factor in the recognition of open intelligence is that open intelligence is equally present in *all* thinking—pleasant thinking *and* disturbing thoughts. Trying to get into a pleasant state is not what open intelligence is.

Data are all equally self-presentations of open intelligence, and no matter their description, they pose no promise and they pose no threat. They are not threatening, nor are they something that is going to provide us comfort and well-being. The only place we'll ever find ultimate comfort and well-being is in open intelligence.

DIRECT EXPERIENCE OF CONFIDENCE
IN OPEN INTELLIGENCE

"It was so clear to me that there was something about me that I hadn't been familiar with, and that it—experientially—was the nature of my existence. For me, the disturbing states were very predominant at first, and so I could see that these states appeared and disappeared in complete relief and relaxation. There wasn't anything I needed to do about them. The idea of feeling that I needed to do something about them kept me tangled up in knots. But I came to see that these disturbing states were self-freeing, self-releasing and spontaneously resolving in this sense of great relief that was at the basis of everything. So, again and again I would return to short moments as much as I could.

With my total commitment to that, very quickly I started to recognize open intelligence—an intelligence that I didn't really even call anything. I just was smarter. I was smarter in relation to myself; I was smarter in relation to all situations. There was a quiet knowing that was at the basis of everything. I began to see this in relation to my own data as they appeared.

Shortly before, I had been miserable due to these disturbing states, but now I was experiencing them as appearing within a great sense of relief and relaxation. There was a quiet but piercing knowing, as well as an absolute clarity about the nature of everything. It's simple, clear and directly accessible for everyone. It is fundamental and basic to everyone's experience."

THE BENEFITS FROM SHORT MOMENTS
OF OPEN INTELLIGENCE

There are immense benefits that come from short moments of open intelligence, repeated many times. One benefit is complete mental and emotional stability. In open intelligence, there is profound intelligence and we are introduced to it right on the spot, wherever we are. It's this simple: if we do not rely on open intelligence, we never find this special intelligence. However, by the power of open intelligence, we find that this unique intelligence includes complete mental and emotional stability, clarity, insight, compassion, natural ethics and beneficial skillfulness in all situations.

The results of short moments of unending open intelligence are very powerful. We as a global human culture have finally tapped into a form of knowledge that can give us complete mental and emotional stability, clarity, insight, compassion, natural ethics and beneficial skillfulness in all situations. With the Internet and telecommunications available today, this is the first time in history that everyone can know this, and we are demonstrating its power together.

ONE SIMPLE CHANGE

CHAPTER TWO

"We choose for open intelligence to be obvious to us or not. Moment-to-moment open intelligence is the most important choice we will ever make."

Confidence in open intelligence is strengthened through the practice of short moments of open intelligence, repeated many times. By virtue of that, certainty about open intelligence is gained in your own experience. By the power of short moments, many times, you come to rely on what is genuine, authentic, authoritative and convincing within you. Then, life becomes a lot easier.

When you emphasize open intelligence rather than data, you open up to the great unifying ground of peace and open intelligence that is the same for everyone. Wherever you are, by the power of gaining confidence in open intelligence, you are automatically being beneficial. First you are beneficial to yourself, and then by the power of open intelligence, you're automatically beneficial to others. You start to really care—about yourself and about everyone—in a very natural way.

No matter what appears, it has no nature independent of open intelligence. Nothing has ever existed independently, separate or apart from this basic state. To take short moments of open intelligence is to allow everything to rest. In allowing everything to rest in open intelligence, it becomes obvious that everything is inseparable from the basic state and is a source of well-being and ease.

It all begins with recognizing open intelligence within yourself. Then you become convinced that open intelligence for everyone is possible. There is no other way. Short moments of open intelligence, repeated many times, become obvious and continuous. We choose for open intelligence to be obvious to us or not. Moment-to-moment open intelligence is the most important choice we will ever make.

The openness of open intelligence gradually brings the discovery of innate warmth towards others and the desire to be of benefit to them. We discover this by the power of relying on open intelligence—the one simple change that makes life easy. There is nothing else that need be done about data streams. All data are naturally clear. We rely on the power of open intelligence in our everyday life.

SIMPLY RELAX

Data are countless, ceaseless and unpredictable. If you try to base well-being on rearranging or controlling the flow of data, you'll be lost in an endless world of labels and descriptions. Simply relax. Relax body and mind completely, no matter what datum appears. Everything is totally free in the perception of it. Everything provides us with a simple choice: to recognize open intelligence or not.

It's nice to have a simple way of talking about who we are that everyone can share within a common understanding. This is all part of keeping it simple. When we learn to complicate things, that's just what we've learned. The more we relax, again and again, we see that open intelligence provides us with perfect spontaneous intelligence in all circumstances.

SIMPLE SOLUTION

Everything you think of, every emotion you have, every sensation, and all other experiences are simply data appearing in open intelligence. The more you think about it, the less you'll instinctively realize it. There's not a single thing to think about. Keep it totally simple. If you do, you'll end up smiling a lot! That's why the instruction is short moments, many times, until it is continuous. The solution is so simple, why not try it?

COMPLETE RELIEF

CHAPTER THREE

"The first time we make the choice to rely on open intelligence rather than emphasizing data, we sense the power of the complete relief to be found in open intelligence."

At the very moment data form, rely on open intelligence—serene and spacious. By the power of relying on open intelligence, its recognition becomes increasingly obvious, and data vanish naturally, like a line drawn in water. By repeatedly relying on short moments of open intelligence, many times, it becomes obvious and continuous. There is no need to alter the flow of data.

Because of the habit of emphasizing data, the initial brief moments of open intelligence may not last long at first; they may almost immediately slip away. In other words, there may be no real stability. "Many times" means that we need to grow more and more confident in open intelligence by repeating the short moment. This is a key point in gaining confidence. The heart of the matter can be captured in the phrase: "short moments, many times, become obvious and continuous"

We find that emphasizing data streams provides only temporary relief—it is never a permanent solution. We learn that it is possible to gain assurance in open intelligence and to live life based on its inherent intelligence, love and satisfaction.

By persisting in this one simple choice, we see benefits from the outset. The first time we make the choice to rely on open intelligence rather than emphasizing data, we sense the power of the complete relief to be found in open intelligence.

Thoughts, emotions, sensations and all other data are simply appearing in open intelligence. Each datum follows another, appearing and resolving in open intelligence. There is no need to try to alter their flow. Like a line drawn in the sky, they leave no trace.

The power of open intelligence shows us that thoughts, emotions, sensations and experiences are simply data within open intelligence. This can be illustrated by the way planets and stars appear within the expanse of space. Similarly, data— thoughts, emotions, sensations and experiences—appear within open intelligence. And just like space is unaffected by any event within it, open intelligence is unaffected by its data.

The openness of space can be likened to our very own open intelligence. We become certain of open intelligence's power to be unaffected by data and to provide a very special kind of intelligence that shows us what to do and how to act in all situations. This means we have greater intelligence and the know-how to use that intelligence to be of benefit. Initially, we know how to use open intelligence to benefit ourselves. We empower ourselves with short moments. As we do so, unending open intelligence becomes obvious.

We rely on open intelligence and begin to relax with all the data sets of daily life. This is done by relying on short moments of open intelligence, repeated many times, until it becomes continuous. By the power of this simple practice we begin to recognize that open intelligence and data are inseparable, like the sky and the color blue.

Due to the potent benefit found in short moments, we naturally commit to open intelligence. The natural presence of open intelligence is automatically enlivened in all daily activity due to our growing familiarization and confidence. Gradually instinctive open intelligence becomes stable and obvious.

Through the power of short moments, repeated many times, distraction by data is replaced with the ease, warmth and clarity of open intelligence. We begin to live a more fulfilling and satisfying life.

As we recognize our natural state of perfection just *as it is*, all effort to "find open intelligence" gradually ceases, and open intelligence is permanent and obvious at all times. It is predominant in the natural flow of all data day and night and is realized to be the natural, uninterrupted flow of all data that appear.

When short moments of open intelligence are repeated many times, recognition becomes obvious and uninterrupted. It is found to be stable in itself. Open intelligence is self-maintained amidst the flow of data. Then, if the recognition of open intelligence slips away, we simply repeat it again. Short moments, repeated many times, lead to spontaneous confidence in open intelligence.

Let the present datum be *as it is*. There is no need to modify it. There is no need to correct it. This is the key to release the tremendous energy and the powers of natural perfection: short moments of open intelligence, many times, become obvious and continuous. Data is simply allowed to be *as it is*—the dynamic creativity of open intelligence that is free in its own place. Unchanging open intelligence is your vantage. It is the easy way to live.

Relying on
Open Intelligence
CHAPTER FOUR

"The emphasis on data is replaced with the ease of relying on open intelligence, and we begin to live a more fulfilling and satisfying life. We find a powerful intelligence that is only available in open intelligence."

When we stop for a moment and consider our life, how much of it has been running from one experience to another hoping to find some kind of comfort? An example of this might be getting up in the morning: we don't feel good or we feel foggy, so we run for a cup of coffee or some kind of experience to change how we feel. Then we look at the people we live with and start thinking about their shortcomings, or we feel guilty because we're thinking about their shortcomings and try to relieve ourselves of that by being nice to them, and so on.

By the time we have to go to work, we're already exhausted! We have to face all these people that we have absolutely no control over and usually can't get along with. Not knowing what to do, we essentially feel powerless and helpless. All day at work we're thinking about somewhere else we'd rather be.

When we do get off work, it might not be any better. We think, "I'll have a drink or a joint, or I'll watch TV or go to a movie or try out that new restaurant"—all the time seeking a positive experience. Then, of course, there's always sex. Nothing else is working, so how about our old standby to provide a moment of complete relief?

We may have controlled, avoided, become attached to or reacted to people, places, things and circumstances in an attempt to find happiness. We may have isolated ourselves and avoided contact with people or circumstances, hoping problems would go away. We may have juggled data, hoping they would provide relief. These may include relationships, romance, work, entertainment, food, money, sex, alcohol and other drugs.

No matter what we did, we never found the complete and long lasting relief that was sought. We may have found that emphasizing our data provided only temporary relief and never provides permanent well-being.

We can test in our experience that it is possible to gain confidence in open intelligence and to rely on its inherent wisdom, love and happiness, rather than on data. By the power of short moments of open intelligence, many times, it becomes obvious, and we find relief from focusing on data.

TRUE COMPASSION FOR OURSELVES AND OTHERS

Positive, negative and neutral data seem to have a power of their own. Moreover, the assumption is that our well-being is dependent on these data sets. This causes turmoil and confusion, because we are constantly trying to emphasize data that we assume will make our situation better. When we emphasize data, we believe they are powerful in their own right.

To instinctively rely on open intelligence is to know that data have their origin in open intelligence and do not have a separate, independent nature. All data are the dynamic energy of open intelligence.

To constantly emphasize data is to choose between one and another by accepting or rejecting one over the other. We decide there are some data we want to keep and others we want to avoid. This throws us into wanting to hold onto positive data and to get rid of negative data—neither of which is possible.

It is important to understand the dynamic of belief in data so we will be able to rely on open intelligence when data appear and not be blindsided by them. When we emphasize data, we suffer from our assumption that they have independent power. It is difficult to gain confidence in open intelligence until it is specifically understood how the process of emphasizing data works in our own day-to-day experience.

By relying on open intelligence we give up the right to be a victim of data. When short moments of open intelligence are repeated many times, the recognition of open intelligence becomes obvious and uninterrupted. It is found to be stable in itself. By the power of open intelligence, we are not distracted by trying to control the flow of data. Then, when the recognition of open intelligence slips away, we simply repeat it again. Short moments, repeated many times, leads to assurance in open intelligence.

RELY ON OPEN INTELLIGENCE

The emphasis on data streams is replaced with the ease of relying on open intelligence, and we begin to live a more fulfilling and satisfying life. We find a powerful intelligence that is only available in open intelligence.

It is important to understand that all data are appearances of open intelligence. Data are unpredictable, countless and ceaseless, arising spontaneously as the display of open intelligence. Whatever our own circumstantial data may be, it is possible for us to rely on open intelligence and no longer be disturbed by their appearance.

We begin to learn the basic premise of relying on open intelligence rather than emphasizing data. We do this for short moments, many times, until it becomes spontaneous. We find that the solution to trying to control the unpredictable flow of data is our fundamental capacity to rely on open intelligence.

NATURAL HEARTFELT BENEFIT

The more confidence we gain in open intelligence, the more we are able to be of profound benefit in all circumstances, but it doesn't require any effort. So, what do we want? A life based on the confusion of believing that data have an independent nature, or a life grounded in the open intelligence and ease of the basic state? There will never be a point we reach where we feel we have satisfied ourselves or anyone else, because the whole game of trying to find happiness and satisfaction by rearranging our data is like trying to find a drink of water in a mirage—constantly looking for something that can never be found.

It's a matter of what we choose and what we place as a priority above all else. If we keep placing personal wants and all our ideas about what we need to make us happy as a priority, then we'll spend our whole life on that hamster wheel, always seeking after the next datum we think will bring us happiness.

Permanent well-being and ease in all circumstances will never be found in re-arranging the circumstances and descriptions of our lives. One of the things to ask ourselves is, "Where have my ideas led me? Do I have complete peace of mind at all times? Am I living a life that is of great benefit to myself and others?"

In each moment we can either choose to emphasize open intelligence or not. Relying on open intelligence for short moments, many times—rather than relying on conventional expectations—provides real sustenance. This will provide us something we can always count on, no matter what kind of situation we are in.

Short moments, many times.

SHORT MOMENTS, MANY TIMES

CHAPTER FIVE

"We acknowledge open intelligence in an uncontrived way, moment-to-moment. We become convinced of the efficacy and power of open intelligence by its results in our life."

We rely on a short moment of open intelligence. As we repeat these short moments again and again, open intelligence becomes continuous. "Continuous" means short moments of open intelligence are no longer required; it is obvious all the time. In a short moment of open intelligence, there is no need to control the flow of data.

When we rely on short moments of open intelligence, what we are really doing is acknowledging open intelligence as the sole source and support of every single naturally occurring moment. This is something we can't possibly understand with intellectual constructs, descriptive frameworks or reference points. This is why short moments, repeated many times, is so important, because it guarantees us the naturalness of what is instinctively authentic in our own direct experience.

We acknowledge open intelligence in an uncontrived way, moment-to-moment. We become convinced of the efficacy and power of open intelligence by its results in our life. There wouldn't be any other way for us to become convinced: our confidence grows when we see the results of open intelligence in our own lives.

CONVICTION WILL DAWN

When something appears—whether it's a thought, emotion, sensation or experience—rather than getting involved in the story about that experience, the choice is made to rely on open intelligence and to acknowledge open intelligence rather than getting involved in all the descriptions and ideas that have been used to describe everything. That is one way of practicing short moments, repeated many times.

Another approach that people use is simply listening to the trainings and reading the books. By listening to the free downloads repeatedly and reading the texts, conviction will dawn. When we say "conviction will dawn," what that means is that open intelligence becomes more and more obvious simply by hearing, reading or being exposed to the trainings in that way.

Some people combine both approaches: short moments during one's daily walk, but also listening to the downloads, reading the books and participating in the trainings. All of these approaches are fine; whatever works for you is perfect, and whatever is increasing your assurance in open intelligence is the right approach. If you are one of these people who can just listen to the talks and open intelligence becomes more and more obvious to you, then that is great.

For most people there is an introduction to open intelligence, and then open intelligence becomes more and more obvious throughout day and night over a period of time. There is no particular instruction about how or when to take short moments; we simply do so whenever we naturally remember.

If we have been living an ordinary life and are introduced to open intelligence—whether it comes about slowly, quickly or in between—there is going to be an adjustment to this new, easeful way of being. We have been conducting ourselves in one way, and suddenly we have all kinds of beneficial qualities and activities that are available to us that we had not previously known. In a very practical way we gradually become accustomed to those skillful means that are evident in open intelligence. This, too, comes about in a very uncontrived, natural way in day-to-day activity.

OPEN INTELLIGENCE

As we go about our ordinary life, we find that we are not as willing to get involved in all the stories about our data. When we don't run off after all the stories to try to describe our life, then our whole approach to life completely alters. We experience everything with increasing openness and ease.

When we are no longer driven by all these stories, then we start to see everything very clearly. Something can come up that has always come up for us, but we are not drawn in that direction anymore. Our natural commitment is to open intelligence, because we have experienced its powerful results. Now we are attracted to open intelligence rather than to our lifetime obsessions. This is more powerful evidence of open intelligence, a balanced view and compassion. In those situations, we save ourselves from the whole story, and we save ourselves from implicating someone else or dragging them into our compulsions of data. Less and less are we interested, because we gain complete assurance in open intelligence.

We gain assurance to the degree that we know that we will be all right, no matter what happens. The power of relying on open intelligence is immense. It clarifies all perceptions. Not only are we going to be all right in life, but we will have well-being at death; we will be able to face death as just another datum.

PRACTICAL RESULTS

Open intelligence is complete perceptual openness in all experience. It is freedom in immediate perception rather than being focused on stories. The whole field of perception opens up in open intelligence to include all perceptions. We may find ourselves having a lot of thoughts and a lot of emotions—even very strong emotions that we could have never tolerated before we began gaining confidence in open intelligence. Confidence is gained through instinctive recognition. It is not gained through thinking about open intelligence or through reasoning. It is gained by the direct perception that all data are inseparable from open intelligence.

When we gain assurance in open intelligence, it has practical results on all levels of living. When we see the power of open intelligence, we are simultaneously seeing our own power to benefit ourselves as that power unleashes well-being within us that we never knew was possible. This self-benefit that is so evident in us very naturally evolves into the desire to want to benefit others.

For most of us, the way we live really changes. We find that we want to contribute in some way that will make things easier for people to live their life. Whether we are inventing new things, working as a caregiver or baking bread, we have clarity, wisdom and compassion when we go about whatever it is we are doing. We see ways of doing things that no one has ever seen before. We become so convinced through seeing the result in our own life that we know it will work for anyone who adopts it. In this way, we benefit all beings everywhere simply by gaining confidence in open intelligence ourselves.

COMPLETE CONFIDENCE IN OPEN INTELLIGENCE

CHAPTER SIX

"After the introduction to open intelligence, it's very important to commit to short moments of open intelligence as often as we remember. Short moments, repeated many times, become obvious and continuous."

Once open intelligence is identified as the source of experience, there is more and more openness that is noticed in one's daily experience. Open intelligence is the source of all experience and is inseparable from all data. It offers us something that we haven't found anywhere else in our life, and it's something that we can count on. With short moments of open intelligence we come to see that there is a continuous soothing energy present throughout all daily activities. We see that we can rely on open intelligence, no matter what is going on.

It is in our practical day-to-day experience that we gain confidence in open intelligence. More and more we rely on our own direct experience of open intelligence and instinctive open intelligence, rather than focusing on our opinions or the opinions of others.

Gradually and very profoundly we increasingly realize that there's something about us that is totally reliable and a source of great ease and well-being.

After the introduction to open intelligence, we choose to rely on open intelligence. It is a commitment that says, "I choose open intelligence rather than the struggle of believing in all my data. I choose to experience open intelligence for myself in each moment, rather than relying on the multitude of descriptions about each situation."

It can't be contrived, so there is no way to push ourselves into open intelligence by forcing ourselves to be clear for long periods of time. The only way to really gain confidence in open intelligence is through uncontrived short moments.

GAINING ASSURANCE IN OPEN INTELLIGENCE

Through this powerful and natural commitment, complete assurance in open intelligence comes about. In other words, rather than having to make the choice to rely on open intelligence, the confidence becomes so strong that open intelligence is naturally present without needing to rest. That assurance applies to all our experience.

More and more of our experience is gathered up into the instinctive realization of open intelligence. In gaining confidence in open intelligence, the confusion of believing in the independent nature of data is diminished. The commitment is to choose open intelligence rather than the descriptions and opinions that are applied to our experience.

Data are ceaseless, countless and unpredictable, and the only way we can really experience open intelligence is to gain confidence in open intelligence. With the instinctive recognition of open intelligence we see that we don't need to analyze open intelligence for it to be present. It opens us up to a powerful intelligence or super-intelligence that subsumes all ideas in its great perspective.

When we naturally take this perspective, we find that we have tremendous physical, mental and emotional energy that we did not have before. It allows us to tap into a force for good within human society. We reveal in ourselves a basic human goodness and brilliance of intellect—completely beyond anything that can be found within descriptive frameworks. No matter how brilliant the descriptive frameworks are, the perspective of the brilliance of open intelligence completely outshines all of them.

Its certainty, pervasiveness and prevalence are so absolute that it can never be disproved. Confidence in the instinctive recognition of natural perfection is what confidence in open intelligence is. It is assurance in something about us that is instinctive. In other words, it's beyond the descriptions of thought and reason.

OPEN INTELLIGENCE OUTSHINES ALL DATA

To familiarize oneself with open intelligence for short moments is an adventure of great wonder. You start to see that open intelligence outshines all data within it. In the same way that all of infinite space contains everyone and everything, so too, open intelligence contains all data without exception. The more confidence you gain in open intelligence and the more certain you are of it as your own nature and the nature of everything, the more you start to see that you are actually the master of the display of your thoughts and emotions.

It's likely that most of your life you have felt at the whim of your thoughts and emotions to one degree or another. By gaining confidence in open intelligence, you start to see that open intelligence has mastery over all thoughts and emotions. For most people, this is discovered little by little and progress is made gradually. More and more all experience is outshone by the open intelligence and ease of the basic state.

It doesn't matter what you're doing, whether you have a family or not or whether you have a job or not. That doesn't have anything to do with gaining assurance in open intelligence. By gaining confidence in open intelligence, you'll either continue doing your same job and living in the same circumstances, or you'll see greater possibilities in all areas of your life.

We will never have the courage or the capacity to go beyond descriptive frameworks as long as we're operating within them. We can't possibly know what we are capable of in terms of our strengths, gifts and talents as long as we restrict ourselves with conventional ideas. As we gain confidence in open intelligence, we'll find that it's easier to do whatever it is we are doing. We'll see more interesting ways of approaching all of our tasks in all aspects of our lives.

OPEN INTELLIGENCE AND COMPASSION

We find the natural warmth, perfection, compassion, spontaneity and intelligence that is present within the natural flow of all data. Each datum is an equal appearance of open intelligence so there is no special datum to look for. All the data of the here-and-now are what open intelligence *is*. By the power of short moments of open intelligence, repeated many times, special data are no longer of particular interest.

It is very important at the start not to push ourselves too hard and to simply rely on open intelligence for short moments, many times. We must remember that the fundamental purpose of short moments, many times, is to realize, maintain and develop continuity of open intelligence. We simply rely on open intelligence rather than emphasizing data.

With the groundwork of short moments, we enter into the recognition of open intelligence as inseparable from data. This happens naturally. It is important to be satisfied with this simple assurance in open intelligence rather than continuing to search for new and better data. It also is important to integrate open intelligence into every situation of ordinary daily life, and this comes about most easily in short moments.

As confidence is gained, we discover that data release spontaneously, and qualities like intelligence and compassion shine forth in open intelligence like the radiance of the sun in the sky.

Short moments, repeated many times, until obvious and continuous, is the direct means for experiencing that all data streams are perfect and inseparable from open intelligence.

TREMENDOUS POWER AND ENERGY

CHAPTER SEVEN

"Through short moments of open intelligence, you will have tremendous power and energy to be of benefit to all, and you will see how profoundly you can be of benefit to yourself. Then you have the thrill of reality where you see how beneficial your life can really be and how much you have to contribute."

A short moment of open intelligence is a short moment of instinctive natural power. Natural power is built in and it is only accessible in open intelligence. It's engineered into every short moment—a short moment that is completely powerful and soothing. The entire flow of data is saturated in this mood of powerful, soothing energy. However, if we try to control the flow of data, we're assuming that there's something wrong with data and that they're not naturally powerful.

What would it be like to *not* regulate the flow of those data? Simply, allow the flow of data within you to be whatever it is. That's what we discover in a short moment of open intelligence.

Many of us are very intent on trying to control our data. All day long we try to control data, and then at the end of the day we collapse in exhaustion. When we take short moments, we start to experience the naturalness and ease that comes about by allowing data to flow on by. This is what it means to have confidence in open intelligence: that no matter what the data are, we don't try to control them. Short moments are repeated many times.

By allowing all of this to be *as it is*, more and more all data sets are recognized to be inseparable from open intelligence—the ground of complete soothing energy.

Completely open intelligence triggers warmth, joy, power and energy. Open intelligence is the source of stability, profound insight, natural ethics, spontaneous motivation to benefit all, skillful activity and the actual power to consistently fulfill beneficial creative intent. Yes, a short moment is completely packed with all of these powers. From the first short moment, these powers are recognized. However, these qualities and abilities go unrecognized when we focus on data. By the power of open intelligence, all is welcomed with complete openness. This automatically cuts through the barriers created by habitual emotional patterns.

The ease of what is right here can never be undone. Everyone and everything is already naturally powerful, regardless of the label or description. This becomes obvious in short moments. The beauty of short moments is that there is increasing confidence, increasing ease and increasing soothing energy, no matter what seems to be occurring in our lives. There's an increasing feeling of *wow* that is very natural. When we realize how easy it is, every datum is seen to be evidence of inherent natural power. Wow! It may take a while to get accustomed to this, but that's okay. Whatever the flow of your everyday life is, it's perfect for this recognition to take place.

The direct experience of everyday life flows easily in open intelligence. There is no need to indulge, renounce, transform, refine or analyze data. Simply let them flow on by rather than trying to alter the course of data. It is open intelligence—the source of the dynamic energy of data—that is emphasized. Nothing need be done about the data.

Relax naturally. This *is* the recognition that all data are naturally present within open intelligence and do not need to be changed. We rely on open intelligence to let data flow along its natural course.

We gradually gain assurance in open intelligence and its power of benefit. The extent and timing of gaining assurance in open intelligence has a pace that is perfect. We learn to trust open intelligence completely.

New situations appear in our life, giving us opportunities to either repeat the same old responses or to rely on open intelligence. An interesting adventure unfolds. Data are unpredictable, so it is impossible to know what the next one will be. Life becomes wondrous when we emphasize open intelligence rather than data. We become resilient and confident, able to laugh at our data, and to be responsive, beneficial and wise.

When we start to gain assurance in open intelligence, we increasingly recognize that data are the natural power of indestructible open intelligence. We place full confidence in indestructible open intelligence rather than in data.

We simply rest the need to get involved in the flow of data, whenever we remember to do so. By the power of our commitment to short moments, we will definitely gain confidence in open intelligence. Data do not have the power to distract us, and with the recognition of open intelligence, confidence is ensured.

Open intelligence is naturally perfect and filled with beneficial qualities and activities. We are introduced to this natural perfection through our experience of the benefits of gaining assurance in open intelligence.

Once we have been introduced to open intelligence, then we are satisfied with that and only need skillful ways to gain greater assurance. Actually, the introduction to open intelligence is the ultimate goal. Then all that there really is left to do is rely on open intelligence and its natural power that is of benefit to all.

We tap into our innate strengths, gifts and talents. This is part of the shift from obsessive self-centered concern into the openness, ease and balanced view of open intelligence.

We have tremendous energy to be of benefit to all. We see how beneficial our life can really be and how much we have to contribute. We see that it's possible to contribute in a relaxed way from a very profound level of intelligence that is completely at ease and that has nothing to prove. It's very simple.

The essence of all data is open intelligence, which is synonymous with natural power. The true nature of all data is equalness. There is not a single thing that is separate from the expanse of that equalness. The scope of open intelligence is a single space of evenness in which everything is equal.

NATURAL POWER

CHAPTER EIGHT

---

*"Natural power manifests in all phenomena
and is not affected by their appearance. All
remains spontaneously in natural power."*

The nature of phenomena is unified within natural perfection and power. Each phenomenon has no independent nature. Like endless sky, it is equal to the vast expanse of open intelligence.

The great unity of phenomena is innate rather than conceptually attained. Natural perfection manifests in all phenomena and is not affected by their appearance. Natural perfection outshines the need to create perfectibility, through emphasizing the rearrangement of appearances. All remains spontaneously in natural perfection. This instinctive understanding or knowingness is equal to open intelligence.

The primacy of open intelligence is native in all experience. Intrinsically there is spontaneous appearance, flowering and self-release of the here-and-now. This is ensured by the obviousness of open intelligence in all experience. There is no diversity in the great variety of phenomena. As no phenomenon can be found to have an independent nature, all are free of their naturally occurring descriptive frameworks and are an expanse of equalness and evenness. Natural perfection shines forth in all phenomena whatsoever.

As all phenomena have no independent nature, their natural perfection is primordially perfect from the beginningless beginning. Natural perfection is an ineffable openness that is spontaneously present and indivisible. It is the space of space, the light of light and the energy of energy. Natural perfection is present in phenomena, and phenomena are present in natural perfection. There is no natural perfection that is separate or apart from phenomena, and there are no phenomena that are separate or apart from natural perfection. The natural perfection of phenomena is like pure space pouring into pure space, or bright light pouring into bright light.

The space of natural perfection is aware. Open intelligence is aware. There is no separate or independent intelligence that ever occurs within natural perfection. Indestructible open intelligence—the all-encompassing view—is present in all of its appearances.

In all thoughts, emotions, sensations and experiences, it is open intelligence that is unavoidably present. Open intelligence is simply *as it is*. It is never distracted nor affected by appearances, including birth, life and death, waking, dreaming and sleeping. Upon the appearance of human birth, life and death, there is simply the basic space of natural perfection—the glorious and spontaneous self-release of the here-and-now. There is no change in natural perfection. It is as it has always been—light in light, natural perfection in natural perfection.

All experience is spontaneously outshone by open intelligence. This is similar to bright sunlight suddenly outshining all the planets and stars that had been evident at night. The appearance of being someone who is imprisoned in a space-time continuum slips away without any notice. No conceptual support is necessary. All the stories of an independent personal identity are no more compelling than a light-hearted fantasy tale. What seemed so before, now is not! A smile of great relief simply continues on as the pure pleasure of open intelligence.

It is clear that open intelligence has always known what it is, and there never has been a time of confusion or non-recognition. As there never has been non-recognition, there never has been an opposed framework of recognition, nor anyone who recognized it or did not recognize it. There never has been an imagined self-identity, thus there is no eventual release from what cannot be found to exist. In the appearances of natural perfection, there is no one to realize something, no effort, and nothing to change. All appearances are equal to the vast expanse of lucid open intelligence.

Natural power binds everything together in luminous open intelligence. Luminosity arises spontaneously and is inseparable from open intelligence like the sky is inseparable from its luster.

Open intelligence rests in itself. How marvellous! Open intelligence plays at resting in itself. This is the direct introduction to open intelligence: self-arising potent qualities and abilities, love and tremendous power.

Great benefit! Great stability! Great well-being!

PERFECT MENTAL AND
EMOTIONAL STABILITY

CHAPTER NINE

"By the power of open intelligence at all times, there is complete mastery over all mental and emotional states. The result guarantees immediate and long-term benefit."

Mental and emotional stability come about through open intelligence in the immediacy of perception. There is complete perceptual openness in all experience. Open intelligence is the beneficial power and energy that overcomes micromanagement of thinking, emotions, sensations and other experiences. As long as these states are micromanaged, there is the belief that well-being will come from this micromanagement. However, well-being comes from open intelligence, rather than from contriving actions to regulate experiential states.

Micromanagement of thoughts and emotions is tense, hyper-vigilant and suffocating. It is based in indulgence, avoidance or replacement of negative states. Neutral states are ignored, positive states are hoped for. When positive states arise there is an attempt to hold onto them and a fear that they will disappear. However, in simply not doing anything when they appear—in letting everything be *as it is*—a resource of perfect insight, profound intelligence, mental and emotional stability, empathy and exceptional skillfulness opens up.

Superior insight into the nature of all situations is beyond indulging, avoiding or replacing the urges and surges of mental, emotional and physical states. Instead, there is pervasive open intelligence throughout all experience. There is no boundary line anywhere, since open intelligence and insight pervade every single situation. There is instinctive recognition of the powerful open intelligence that pervades all states. This open intelligence is where everything stands or falls. In open intelligence is the capacity of letting everything that takes place be liberated within its spaciousness and expansiveness.

As long as experiential states are micromanaged on a moment-to-moment basis, intelligence is limited to the arena of experience. When thoughts and emotions are allowed to be as they are, a vast expanse of open intelligence and energy spontaneously arises. Suddenly, there is a wide range of solutions that never existed before.

The most important choice in every moment is this choice: open intelligence or micromanagement of experience. It is only in allowing experience to be *as it is* that it spontaneously self-releases in radiant open intelligence. By the power of instinctive recognition of open intelligence, its empowering atmosphere of beneficial power and energy are released and become evident in all situations.

By the power of open intelligence, we see that experience vanishes naturally in and of itself. It is self-freeing. It spontaneously self-releases, like the flight path of a bird in the sky or a line drawn in water or like mist evaporating in air. Experience is non-independent of open intelligence. It does not have any kind of individual self-generated power of its own. It is open intelligence that is the supreme unifying intelligence and the only fuel of experience. All experience is fuelled by the extreme well-being of the continuum of open intelligence.

By the power of instinctive open intelligence, there is a tremendous release of the beneficial power and energy of complete spontaneity. There is extremely powerful intellectual and emotional freedom.

What could be a greater relief than to stop trying to fix thoughts and emotions? In this way, the discovery is made that open intelligence is completely amazing, so powerful, so effective and efficient in every situation. All circumstances are without impediment. And, all of this comes about by just allowing everything to be *as it is*. This brings micromanagement of all kinds to a complete halt.

By the power of open intelligence at all times, there is complete mastery over all mental and emotional states. The result guarantees immediate and long-term benefit. In instinctive open intelligence, there is the ability to easily and effortlessly empower ourselves and others to be the best that we can be.

Optimal innovation and benefit require perfect mental and emotional stability. Swiftly and surely it becomes evident through the practice of short moments of open intelligence, repeated many times, until open intelligence is continuous at all times. Short moments is like a lightning bolt that strikes experience with illuminating intelligence and stability.

NATURAL ETHICS

CHAPTER TEN

"True ethics is deep caring, connection and intimacy with everyone and everything and a responsiveness to that in our actions. Wishing everyone well, feeling compassionate, wanting to be of benefit—it's all part of who you are already!"

The data that are appearing right now are all a perfect opportunity to recognize open intelligence. We've always been perfect, and we've always been okay. Short moments, many times is so simple, because we see that there's nothing to avoid, nothing to defend against and nothing to control. Whatever data are, they're naturally perfect.

Once we start to instinctively recognize the natural perfection of everything exactly *as it is* right here, it doesn't matter what we're thinking or what our emotions, sensations or experiences are. We allow all data to be *as they are* without controlling that flow.

It is of no concern what the conventional ideas are about how all these data sets came about. As much as the impulse might be to examine data, there is no intelligence in examining data. The only real intelligence is in short moments of open intelligence; it is not in examining data streams.

By resting with all of your own data you start to experience deep compassion for what you've put yourself through in terms of believing in data. When you have that for yourself, then you instantaneously feel it for everyone.

There's no reason to try to control the flow of data. There isn't anything in any datum that is other than completely open love, open intelligence and energy. We have learned to try to regulate data, but they've never needed to be regulated. The only reason we might have a datum of tension or feeling like things aren't okay is because we've learned to try to control our thoughts and emotions. We've also learned that if we don't control our thoughts and emotions, it will be very, very scary.

Many of us try so hard to have people look at us in only one way, and we try to watch everything we do so that people will like us, but all these are data. There is absolutely nothing to protect in openness.

Whatever your data are, they are the source of open intelligence's power. Everyone is always looking for caring, intimacy and connection, and that's where caring, intimacy and connection are: in the natural flow of your own data and in all the hideous thoughts and emotions that you are sure will crush you. That's where total love, power, beauty and energy is! It's in the data that are unbearable for you to have. There's no way to control the flow anyway, so relax and know that you'll get more and more accustomed to this.

Love, caring and intimacy are already present in open intelligence as well as the energy to really have good relationships with other people. Return again and again to that open intelligence—that is all that is required.

A DEEP CARING FOR ALL

Reliance on open intelligence brings a deep understanding of the condition of humankind as well as a very deep compassion and a very deep sense of wishing everyone well. When you begin to gain confidence in open intelligence, you see that it really is the solution that provides well-being in every moment.

When you experience this for yourself, you naturally wish that for everyone.

It's only when we come into allowing everything within us to be *as it is* and allowing everything external to be *as it is* that we're really able to be free of everything in the immediacy of perception. Then we're able to connect intimately with everyone and everything. If we allow all of our own data to be exactly as they are, then we'll be able to understand other people in a truly intimate way. We'll be able to connect in a real and fundamental way with other human beings. By the power of short moments of open intelligence, repeated many times, we start to experience what it means to be truly connected to ourselves and others. We connect with what we really are, and we connect with other people.

True ethics is this deep caring, connection and intimacy with everyone and everything and a responsiveness to that in our actions. When we go out into the world and look at people, no one anywhere is a stranger. This is really what we want. It's so natural, simple and easy. Full-blown compassion is in open intelligence, but we have to stay with short moments of open intelligence, repeatedly, in order to make it obvious and real for ourselves.

Wishing everyone well, feeling powerful, caring, ethical and skillful, wanting to be of benefit—it's all part of who you are already! By the very power of relying on open intelligence, there are more and more prolonged periods of open intelligence throughout the day, until your whole life is consumed by open intelligence's powerful qualities and activities. You come to realize that you've never really had any other way of looking at things—you just thought you did. What you could say is that to not recognize open intelligence is a misperception—that's all. It's a mistake that can be easily corrected.

Return again and again to that brief moment of total open intelligence that is the essence of every perception, and in so doing you will discover naturally occurring love, caring and ethics which end misperception.

Short moments is the direct method and the skillful means that allows everyone to attain the complete natural ethics, caring, mental and emotional stability, love, tremendous energy and open intelligence that are present within every human being.

It's like being the ultimate mother and father to yourself. It's being that gentle, powerful and commanding with yourself, where there isn't any violence whatsoever. It is as if you had a little child that you adored and you could only see its beauty and power, nothing else—no matter what other people said. That's how you fall in love with yourself: where you always see the increasing beauty, power, and vitality.

OPEN INTELLIGENCE

CHAPTER ELEVEN

"Natural open intelligence pervades every-thing."

Short moments of open intelligence, repeated many times reveal natural ease and openness within everything. Short moments are taken until open intelligence becomes obvious. Open intelligence is inseparable from everything that app-ears.

Short moments acknowledges again and again, the fundamental condition of every perception you are having as inseparable from pervasive open intelligence. By acknowledging open intelligence as the root of all data and relying on open intelligence for short moments, eventually the ease of open intelligence pervades all experience, and there is no need to take short moments any longer.

If a painful perception comes up and you start elaborating on it, this is going to lead to all kinds of other thoughts about it. If you were standing in a muddy pond and wanted the pond to be clear, you would not stir the water with a stick. You would stand still until all the mud naturally settled out. The same is true with perceptions. When we allow perceptions to be by simply relying on open intelligence for short moments repeated again and again, it becomes clear that all perceptions are settled in and of themselves with nothing needing to be done. All data are pervaded with open intelligence.

By repeatedly relying on this inherent open intelligence, you come to see that you are not overwhelmed by any data—and you never have been! Thinking that you have been overwhelmed by ideas or descriptions is merely another datum.

When belief in any data starts to trouble you, rely on short moments of open intelligence instead.

Getting into descriptions and allowing them to trouble you is exhausting and painful. To indulge in descriptions, *or* to enjoy a moment of open intelligence—that is a very fundamental choice. Are you going to go for the pain, or are you going to enjoy the stability and power of open intelligence? Committing to the instinctive recognition of stable open intelligence has to be a priority above all else. By making it a priority above all else, you are able to truly come into the confidence of the instinctive recognition of inherent natural perfection, which is a reality of total power and relief at all times.

IT'S UP TO YOU AND IT'S UP TO ME

Open intelligence takes each here-and-now all the way, open intelligence subsumes worry and concern. Open intelligence's sovereignty is comprehensive. The first moment that you choose open intelligence rather than the pain of a described reality, it's a moment of total open intelligence where you can say, "Wow, being troubled by worry is optional. It's not up to other people, places or things—it's up to me, nobody else!" Based upon that realization, it's possible to enjoy the courage and power of relying on open intelligence again and again.

Being troubled by descriptive labels is actually a lucky thing, because it provides great motivation towards wanting to get out of that prison. In relying on short moments, repeatedly, we choose open intelligence over the confusion of descriptions again and again. This simple choice can be taken in every moment. It is entirely up to you.

All powerful qualities and activities already are in each short moment. You can count on this without fail. Nothing else is needed. Take every opportunity you can to optimize open intelligence. Open intelligence is the greatest support. Rely on those who have gained confidence in open intelligence before to support you. Rely on the Four Mainstays. This makes open intelligence easy for everyone. Everyone is included. No one is left out.

NATURAL OPEN INTELLIGENCE, NATURAL POWER

In allowing short moments of open intelligence, natural intelligence will become obvious. In each short moment there's a touching in with the power of natural intelligence. Natural intelligence's potency pervades everything. As we enjoy more powerful open intelligence, we begin to notice that the natural potency of open intelligence is always present and that it isn't a destination we need to reach.

In a short moment of open intelligence, we experience complete openness. Getting a taste of short moments helps us recognize that this openness pervades everything. Open intelligence is a powerfully comfortable space of complete well-being, clarity and ease.

To have complete confidence in open intelligence means that we are completely comfortable with the natural flow of data—and that natural flow includes everything: jealousy, anger, hatred, bliss, desire, fear, everything. However, if we get all caught up in these emotions and don't rely on our own natural open intelligence, then we may act on those things impulsively.

You see what has motivated you to act impulsively, and you see what motivates other people to act impulsively. This is very powerful and is another reason why it's very important not to take what's going on as evidence of lack of open intelligence. Whatever it is, that's what it is. However you are, that's great. Whoever you are, whatever your data are, that's the evidence of natural perfection.

OPEN INTELLIGENCE FOR THE BENEFIT OF ALL

It's not merely open intelligence for the sake of open intelligence; it's open intelligence for the benefit of all. It's very easy to see whether or not the fruits of open intelligence are really in your own experience. You see it in naturally wanting to be of benefit to all, in being naturally helpful and in increasing mental and emotional stability that is evident to you and to others as well. Those things are the evidence and assurance of open intelligence. The power of open intelligence is increasingly obvious and evident throughout life.

Whenever you happen to spontaneously remember short moments of open intelligence, that's okay. Don't try to apply it like a band-aid to a specific situation in order to avoid the situation or replace it. Initially you start to gain assurance in the *uncontrived, spontaneous ever-presence of open intelligence within all data*, then you rely on open intelligence again and again rather than on the descriptions. Rely on open intelligence for short moments threaded throughout your life, and open intelligence will become obvious throughout all of your day.

Short moments of open intelligence, many times, is what you can really count on.

POWERFUL BENEFIT

CHAPTER TWELVE

"In grounding ourselves in open intelligence, there is an incredible power to see all kinds of solutions we couldn't see before and to act powerfully and practically in the world. From the vantage of open intelligence, we're no longer bound within conventional constructs."

Through short moments, many times, we guarantee ourselves uncontrived naturalness. The uncontrived naturalness of open intelligence is a power that is innate in every single human being. As we gain assurance in open intelligence, very naturally and spontaneously our mental, emotional and physical states and the qualities and activities of our life become infused with powerful open intelligence.

How can we act powerfully and beneficially in the world? By the power of short moments of open intelligence, many times until it becomes continuous. Without that we won't be able to help ourselves from having emotional reactions and all kinds of wild and crazy thoughts that will lead us off in many directions. Instead, we ground ourselves in open intelligence and we gain assurance in that open intelligence. Through this, we know how to act skillfully and powerfully in every moment. And, we know that we are going to be okay.

In grounding ourselves in open intelligence, there is an incredible power to see all kinds of things we couldn't see before and to act powerfully in the world. From the vantage of open intelligence, we're no longer bound within conventional constructs. If you are an environmentalist, a doctor, an engineer, a bread baker or whatever you happen to be, you'll have an entirely different perspective than if open intelligence were lacking. From the perspective of open intelligence you will have a power that simply isn't present if there is no confidence in open intelligence. If there are burning issues that are really important to you, you want to act from the clarity that comes from confidence in open intelligence rather than acting based upon the limitations of data. Once there is no limitation of conventional intellectual speculation about how to solve problems, all kinds of new ways of looking at problems open up.

There is tremendous power in the practice of short moments, many times. It's right here.

COMPLETE COOPERATION

In naturally allowing everything to rest in open intelligence repeatedly, we have more and more clarity and compassion. It naturally comes about without any effort. Open intelligence and compassion aren't something we can accumulate or learn. We simply have to allow everything to be *as it is*. Compassion and clarity are spontaneously occurring. They can't be brought about by any means, and in short moments, many times, we recognize that they are already naturally present.

We start to see from the first short moment that these short moments have incredible power. How do we prove that to ourselves? We test it in our own experience. By relying on repeated short moments of inherent open intelligence, we see that emotions and thoughts that used to really trouble us are no longer troubling. We can allow these thoughts and emotions to be *as they are*, rather than feeling we need to do something about them. From the beginning we see that open intelligence is powerful and very beneficial. Indestructible power and benefit are what open intelligence and compassion are. We are empowered with our basic state, and by recognizing and identifying with that basic state for short moments, repeated many times, we come to feel more and more of its practical power in our life.

We come into complete cooperation with ourselves and others. We begin to see that everything abides in a natural state of complete cooperation. Through short moments, we see that right here. Right here! No matter what is appearing in us, it is exactly as it's meant to be. It rests perfectly and beautifully in the natural state and doesn't need to be changed. Short moments, repeated many times, become obvious and continuous.

POWERFUL WELL-BEING
IN EVERY MOMENT
CHAPTER THIRTEEN

"Open intelligence is in harmony with data.
There is no fighting with data anymore. This is
the best well-being."

Open intelligence is continuous, like the seamless sky. Its self-existing nature is like light filling space. Perfect open intelligence is like pure space. When we rest naturally and do not struggle with the natural flow of data, they vanish in powerful open intelligence.

Data streams do not need to be controlled in order to gain assurance in open intelligence. Negative and positive data are the dynamic energy of open intelligence and cannot be found to have an independent nature. Each moment is supported by the powerful current of open intelligence.

Open intelligence is evident and naturally occurring in all data streams, regardless of their description. With an easygoing attitude, like a person who has nothing more to do, rest in whatever way is comfortable, neither tense nor loose. Rest naturally in the carefree well-being of open intelligence.

Disturbing states will not change by trying to avoid them, for data cannot ignore data, like fire cannot be rid of heat. Disturbing states will not change by trying to replace them with positive states, for a datum cannot change a datum, just as an emerald cannot change its color. Data cannot be stilled by forcing them to become calm or analyzing them, for that is none other than descriptions involved in manipulating descriptions. They cannot be freed with antidotes of any kind, for that would be like wanting to make muddy water clearer, yet stirring it with a stick; antidotes, too, are data that are the pure stream of open intelligence. Disturbing states in and of themselves are inseparable from open intelligence, so let them be as they are and just relax.

Open intelligence is in harmony with data. There is no fighting with data anymore. This is the best well-being. Spacious open intelligence naturally allows data to be *as it is*. Everything happens very simply. Since there is no need to change the flow of experience, antidotes and remedies to experience come to a complete stop in the pure space of luminous open intelligence.

Data are a single stream of evenness and equalness that are inseparable from open intelligence like the color blue is inseparable from the sky. There is complete equalness in the single flow of data.

The indivisibility of open intelligence and data bears tremendous energy, deep insight into the nature of everything, and more. Open intelligence and the uniflow of data—like the sun and its rays—is expressed in the natural perfection and benefit of its magnificent qualities and activities that appear in everyday life.

Given that open intelligence is free of the need to alter the natural flow of appearances, it is important to relax and let everything be *as it is*. We are at our most powerful in all daily activities through letting things be as they are. Let all data flow along naturally without trying to alter their course in any way. Fear, anger, data about work, relationship, money, food and sex continue to arise. It is important to know that the arising of these is not evidence of non-recognition of open intelligence. We increasingly understand and recognize that all data streams are open intelligence only.

This gives rise to well-being and joy. The need to rely on open intelligence ends; there is no longer any interval between open intelligence and data. Open intelligence and data do not come together or separate. Although much ado is made about all kinds of things by naming them, we realize that they are nothing but the natural perfection of open intelligence.

Finally, all data are outshone in the pure space of natural perfection. Everything disappears into unified basic space. All sounds disappear upon their arising, like an echo. Appearances disappear like a rainbow vanishing into the sky, and all other data disappear like a line drawn in water. This is the powerful benefit of naturally perfect open intelligence, where there is no longer even the possibility of separate data.

In order to release the powers of the natural perfection of open intelligence, it is important to gain confidence in open intelligence. Simply allow data to be *as it is*—the dynamic energy of open intelligence that is free in its own place. The key to the release of the tremendous energy of wisdom and natural perfection is short moments of open intelligence, repeatedly, until obvious at all times.

In each short moment, warmhearted beneficial intent, compassion, luminous intelligence, wisdom, mental and emotional stability and skillfulness are already present and shining like a great sun. Do not be fooled by believing in anything more complicated than this. By the power of short moments, ensure a peaceful life, and shower kindness everywhere.

This is the pivotal instruction that needs no study: short moments, many times, become continuous. A gift as simple as this belongs to everyone. It is like living on an island of gold where everything is gold. Just so, all moments contain the opportunity of the riches of open intelligence. Open intelligence releases tremendous energy to see everything clearly, like removing a blindfold from the eyes.

Ensure the well-being of yourself and future generations with short moments, many times. All can understand this and come to agreement regardless of belief. In open intelligence, the underlying meaning of all beliefs is understood.

All of the noblest aspirations are contained in open intelligence—the great unifying love-force.

OPEN INTELLIGENCE EQUALS WORLD PEACE

CHAPTER FOURTEEN

"Everyone has within them the aspiration for peace—every single person. When that aspiration comes together with the power of the peace within us that is a most auspicious meeting. That is very fortunate indeed."

Peaceful, powerful open intelligence is the nature of all of our experience. Where is this peace located? In our everyday experience. It isn't anywhere other than that. It is not a special thing that is separate from everything else. It pervades everything. It is very important when we are relying on short moments of open intelligence to have a clear understanding that all of our thoughts, emotions, sensations and experiences are pervaded with the powerful, peaceful ease of open intelligence. Every thought we think, every emotion we have, every action we engage in is timelessly free, organic and filled with powerful, peaceful open intelligence.

In life we learn all about opposites like good and bad, love and hate, so when we first hear about short moments of open intelligence we may think, "Oh great, I can get away from all my negative states," but pretty soon we find out that this isn't what short moments of open intelligence is about at all. It's about recognizing peace *that pervades* everything. We are not trying to get away from anything; rather, we're coming to experience the true nature of everything.

By relying on short moments of open intelligence, we come to the definitive conclusion that everything is united in peace. At that point it is not some kind of made-up intellectual process for us, but our own direct experience. Peace is there when we are suffering incredible emotional heartache and we see that the heartache is inseparable from our peaceful nature, or when we have a devastating physical condition and we see that it too is inseparable from pervasive peace. When this is our direct experience, we increasingly experience that *everything* is pervaded with power and peace.

Peace power equals open intelligence and open intelligence equals peace power. The key point is that in short moments, many times, open intelligence and peace become obvious.

This natural power is an all-abundant vibe. It is the infrastructure of everything. It is the economy that fulfills all beneficial wishes for everyone, the natural resource that is always available. The natural power of open intelligence can completely change our own life and the world. Open intelligence is a call to action, a call to the power of our own nature and our own world. It is up to you, it is up to me, in open intelligence's power there is nothing we cannot be. With the natural resource and power of open intelligence, we can build the world we want to see—together.

INTIMATELY UNITED WITH EVERYONE
AND EVERYTHING

Through short moments of open-hearted open intelligence, repeated many times, we really start to feel intimately united with everyone and everything. That is when we really have the power for the first time to be in relationship with someone else. By the power of short moments, we come to know what real love is all about. We find that the love we've been looking for in somebody or something else is really within us. We could seek it forever in other people, places or things, but would never find it there. Real love is in our inherent peaceful nature. The only way we can really experience this at all times is through the power of short moments.

When we gain assurance in open intelligence, we find a natural way to be in an easeful relationship with everyone. For the first time we become capable of being fully loving and powerfully compassionate.

By relying on open intelligence we find that compassion is inherent in everything, and it doesn't need to be contrived in any way. We find the inherent, organic, uninhibited harmony of everything in short moments, many times.

IRREVERSIBLE POWER AND PEACE

An excellent illustration for open intelligence existing within all of our thoughts, emotions, sensations and other experiences is one of butter existing in cream. When cream is churned, the butter becomes obvious.

Likewise, we can count on short moments of power and peace, repeated again and again. It spontaneously becomes continuous power and peace in all situations. We find irreversible peace at all times.

By the power of short moments, we begin to discover more and more a sense of powerful and peaceful open intelligence that fills us with tremendously motivated energy to benefit all. By carrying on with short moments, whenever we remember to do so, the moments naturally begin to last longer. As the moments of open intelligence grow longer, we find that our mind and body are functioning more powerfully and easily. We begin to notice a powerful quality in our daily life and increasing beneficial energy.

THE POWER OF THIS SIMPLE PRACTICE

We begin to feel, "Wow! This short moments thing is really working!" We start to notice that everything functions more powerfully and easily from the first. Our thoughts and emotions flow on effortlessly. Even if we should experience a total upheaval in some aspect of our life, we have an ease that wasn't there before. We've not only been introduced to our powerful and peaceful nature, but now we're living our powerful and peaceful nature—and we know it's there for us all the time.

THE OPTIMAL WAY OF BEING HUMAN

CHAPTER FIFTEEN

"By the power of open intelligence, the extraordinary energy of basic power is released."

As soothing energy becomes increasingly evident, it is found that in steadfast open intelligence there is a relentless power to be of benefit that never wavers. In the past we may have contrived ways to be of benefit, but in steadfast open intelligence the relentless desire to be of benefit is a natural disposition. It's the way one's life flows when there is no effort. Every other way of doing things slips away. No effort is required for it to be that way, it simply inherently is.

Every short moment of open intelligence is derived from the forever increasing and spontaneous motivation and energy to bring about universal happiness and beneficial circumstances for all. The entire basis of nature itself is spontaneous power, motivation and energy, a spontaneous responsiveness to everyone and everything. When a short moment of open intelligence is relied upon, that is the power source that is tapped into—the power source that is the nature of everything.

This is the life force itself and the basic creativity of open intelligence, which is the innate, radiant energy released by its instinctive realization. The life force itself is how we came to be. It was there before we were, and it's always here with us. When we rely on open intelligence, we come to see that we have an innate radiant and powerful energy that is inseparable from everything about us. Everything about us is the magnificent display of this innate radiant energy and the magnificent home of open intelligence itself.

REACHING THE SUMMIT OF BEING

If you have regrets about the past, rely on open intelligence. If you have regrets about the present, rely on open intelligence. If you have fear about the future, rely on open intelligence. It doesn't matter what's going on; the relief and understanding of what is occurring is found in the recognition of open intelligence. There is no other way to really understand, recognize or realize the nature of what's occurring other than in that brief moment of forever powerful open intelligence.

In open intelligence, without contriving anything, we find mental and emotional stability that is complete, no matter what appears. Natural ethics and caring, amazing skill and wisdom come from the forever unwavering open intelligence that recognizes itself to be equally stable in both tormenting and peaceful data sets. That is true stability.

The encounter with short moments is exceedingly fortunate. Please know how greatly fortunate you are to have ever heard about this. No matter what goes on with your body, voice and mind, open intelligence is entirely stable, indestructible and unchanging. Birth comes, life comes, death comes and your basic state of open intelligence is indestructible. Identify with that about yourself that can never be destroyed and which protects you in all situations.

Guard open intelligence well and it will serve you completely. That is very simple. There is nothing to do. Just relax in potent open intelligence. Whatever you are doing, it is a powerful expression of open intelligence. Connect with the power of open intelligence rather than the definition of the data;

this is the distinction. This is true discernment. Open intelligence is this great power itself in human form.

It is the optimal way of being human.

Never underestimate the power of this simple practice. It is the most powerful force on Earth.

BALANCED VIEW RESOURCES

There are many resources available for anyone who is interested in knowing more about the Balanced View Training. The main information source is our website www.balancedview.org. Posted there are numerous public talks, videos, books and a forum. The forum is a place where people all over the world share their experience of relying on open intelligence in daily life. All video and audio talks are free and can be easily downloaded in mp4 and mp3 format.

Also listed on the www.balancedview.org website is a schedule of Balanced View trainings offered by approved trainers around the world. Venues range from face-to-face trainings and public open meetings, to trainings and meetings offered via teleconference bridge.

The support network of Balanced View—the Four Mainstays—is available 24 hours a day, seven days a week for anyone interested in gaining confidence in open intelligence.

When confidence is inspired by Balanced View's Four Mainstays—1) short moments of open intelligence, 2) the trainer, 3) the training, and 4) the worldwide community—there is increasing instinctive recognition of openhearted, powerful open intelligence until it is continuous at all times. Then there is no longer the possibility of being fooled by appearances of data, not during life and not upon death.

Made in the USA
San Bernardino, CA
12 January 2013